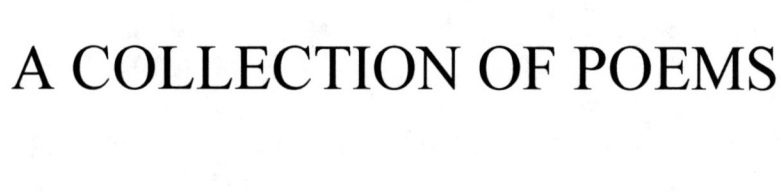

A COLLECTION OF POEMS

where fancy led

A COLLECTION OF POEMS

Jean Boggs Baker

AuthorHouse™
1663 Liberty Drive
Bloomington, IN 47403
www.authorhouse.com
Phone: 1-800-839-8640

© 2011 Jean Boggs Baker. All rights reserved.

No part of this book may be reproduced, stored in a retrieval system, or transmitted by any means without the written permission of the author.

First published by AuthorHouse 6/8/2011

ISBN: 978-1-4634-0019-4 (hc)
ISBN: 978-1-4634-0020-0 (e)
ISBN: 978-1-4634-0021-7 (sc)

Library of Congress Control Number: 2011908713

Printed in the United States of America

Any people depicted in stock imagery provided by Thinkstock are models, and such images are being used for illustrative purposes only. Certain stock imagery © Thinkstock.

This book is printed on acid-free paper.

Because of the dynamic nature of the Internet, any web addresses or links contained in this book may have changed since publication and may no longer be valid. The views expressed in this work are solely those of the author and do not necessarily reflect the views of the publisher, and the publisher hereby disclaims any responsibility for them.

To My Family

'Tis late to dream — to romanticize —
Though fancy beckoned me —
I followed in wonder,
Not knowing what I'd see.

Why, I asked, and whither?
But fancy would not say,
She looked at me whimsically,
And laughing led the way.

jbb

CONTENTS

Foreword xiv
Introduction..xvii
Acknowledgments..xix

I.   Love, Friendship and Family

    Heartbreak 3
    The Follies of Youth 4
    Love's Traitor... 6
    The Concept of Love 7
    A Love Story... 8
    When I Was Feeling Down 10
    Her Letter.. 12
    The Red Shirt... 14
    An Accolade to my Sister, Lee.................... 16
    Echoes of the Past 17
    The Fool... 18
    Love's Sad Song... 19
    The Man I Love and the Man Who Loves Me................ 20
    Change of Heart.. 21
    Champagne Wishes 22
    Rumors 23
    For My Grandson... 24
    The Red Hat Society 25
    A Stricken Heart.. 26
    God's Love 27
    My Mother... 28
    My Dad 29

CONTENTS

    The Varsity Coach 30
    Coal Mining 31
    My Grandson's New Wife 32
    A Great Man 33

II. Childhood and Youth
    Chase 37
    Karly 38
    Lacey 39
    Hugs and Kisses 40
    Olivia 42
    Trace 43
    Trent's Song 44
    Playing Ball 45
    Bowling Baby 46
    The Rose 47
    My Great Grandson 48
    Trent 56
    Wednesday's Child 57

III. Poems Based on True Stories
    The Sheriff's Wife 61
    A Set of Blue Willow 62
    Wedding in Old Charleston 64
    Grandpa Lost 66
    When My Dad Was Young 68

CONTENTS

An Imaginary Friend 70
An Intruder 72
Winter Flood 75
Sitting With Trace.. 78
My Uncle Clay 79
Labor Day Weekend of '54....................................... 80
The Northern Lights (Aurora Borealis) 82
Through Wind and Snow 83
The Dreamer 86
The Accident... 88
Toppled in the Street 90
Her London Experience 92
The Gypsies... 98

IV. Humor and Whimsy
Candles.. 103
Story Things Get All Mixed Up 104
She's Just an Old Maid 105
Sheridan Homer Isaac Tanner................................ 106
Spreading Cheer 107
When Skiing Home 108
The Fisherman 110
Phantoms.. 112
Reflections of the Past 113
Insomnia.. 114
Old Quincy's Son 115

CONTENTS

    Jammin' With the Boys 116

    Saying No 117

    Her Curiosity 118

    Those Golden Years... 119

V.   Different Types of Poems

    A Monorhyme 123

    Haiku Poetry 124

    Summer's Storms 126

    Sunset.. 127

    Depiction of Me.. 128

    The Crescent Moon.. 129

    Shower Power 130

    Springtime's Romance 131

    Diamantes 132

    A Rondel 133

    Terry's Ballad 134

    We'll Inherit the Earth 136

    Dangers Unknown.. 145

    Morning 146

    Whose Heart Fell Captive 148

    Word Play 149

VI. Nature

    The Mighty Mississippi 153

    The Storm.. 156

CONTENTS

Jack Frost 157
Lightning 158
The Great Firestorm 160
Great Balls of Fire 162
Nature's Wrath 163
A Bird Song 164
Indigo Bunting 165
That Cat 166
The Fawn 167
A Little Pond 168
A Grand Old Tree 169
Gusts of Wind 170
Springtime 171
Summer 172
Autumn 174
Autumn Leaves 175
Winter 176
That Blast of Polar Air 177
A Falling Star 178
Rainbow 179
A Double Rainbow 180
Thundersnow 181

VII. Various Themes

A Friendly Stranger 185
Another Birthday 190

CONTENTS

Opposites Entice 186

Faith 187

Multiple Sclerosis 188

The In Between 190

Providence Intervened.. 192

The Past 193

All Alone 194

This Once Stately Home.. 195

Waiting for Mr. Right 196

Birthday Wishes.. 197

A Lady-Killer 198

Every Young Girl's Dream 200

A Spectral Light 202

Birthday Celebration.. 203

With Age... 204

Because.. 205

Nostalgia 206

Index of First Lines.. 209

FOREWORD

Decima Jean Boggs was born at home on the farm in Big Otter, WV, that had belonged to the Boggs family for generations. She was a middle child of six and as you can see from her picture, her fancy had already begun to develop at the young age of four, when she began school life already knowing how to read. After listening to her mother, hour after hour, trying to teach her older brother how to read, she learned this prerequisite for school. Perhaps that's why Jean had only been in school for a few months 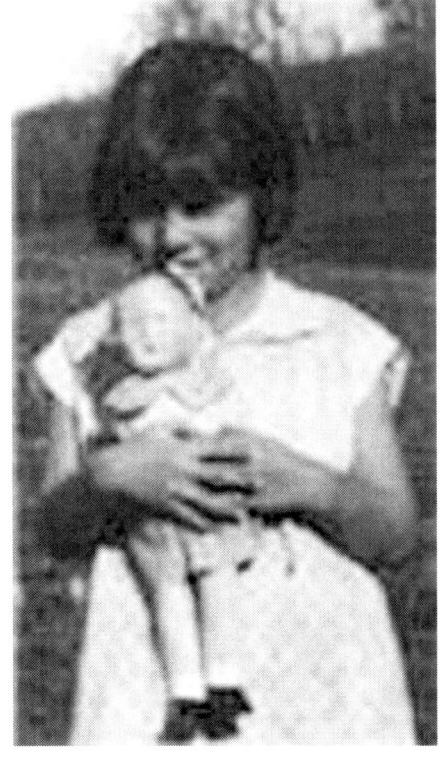 and was double promoted to the fourth grade. She stayed there for a few years until she was able to conserve numbers which one needs to do for the difficult tasks of multiplication and division.

Jean had a passion for reading and would stay up for hours past bedtime trying to get her fill. By kerosene lamp she dreamt, hoping to go undetected which was quite difficult in such a large family.

She used to love going into her grandfather's attic to flightfully while away the hours. It was large enough to have held a ballroom of guests, but after a few minutes of exploring the trunks and treasures; she was quite content to cozy up with an apple in one hand and a book in the other.

Her poem, "The Dreamer," depicts her better than any other my mother has written. This collection may leave you with a little glimpse of her or those she frolicked with throughout her life. Although some of her poems are just her plea to let you see how she might have been inspired by God given things.

It wasn't until her retirement that she started laying down her book from time to time to pick up her pen and paper. Her hope is that you are inspired by fancy, too!

Donna L. Baker

INTRODUCTION

Writing has been a lifelong pursuit and poetry my literary love. I have delighted in many moments caught up in wordplay.

The beauty of poetry is the wide range of emotions one feels while reading a poem. I don't know what you will think or feel as you read; what is important is that you feel!

This book is a collection of poetry with roots in the rolling hills of West Virginia. My poems bloom and blossom from my experiences and imagination. Some of my poems are about family and friends; places I've been and would like to have gone; and people I have met along the way. They are also about imaginary happenings, playing with words and different types of poetry.

I hope that you will share the magical flights with fancy while reading my poetry.

"Winter," was published on the back cover of Country Woman magazine, Jan/Feb 2007. My poems, "A Set of Blue Willow" and "My Uncle Clay," were published in "Now and Then," Volume 18. No. 1, Fall 2007, a quarterly journal of the Clay County (West Virginia) Landmarks Commission and Historical Society.

ACKNOWLEDGMENTS

I would like to thank my family, who has listened and shared, helping to make "Fancy" happen. "Fancy" was a collaborative family effort. My first poem for this book was about my sister. After I wrote the poem, she entered it in a poetry contest. Thanks, Lou! My granddaughters, Lori and Melissa, and their husbands, Drexel and Matthew, helped me find and eliminate some of the flaws. I appreciate your help.

Angela, thank you for the lovely poem, "Opalescent Beauty," that you wrote about me. The Foreword was written by my daughter, Donna. Donna, thank you for inspiring me and keeping me going. The formatting of this book was done by my daughter, Gail. Gail, thank you for tirelessly putting up with the many changes I made along the way. My sister, Leoma, provided me with numerous books on poetry, read my poems, and encouraged me to have them published. My brother, Alan, and his wife, Leanna, found AuthorHouse to publish them. I am truly grateful to all of you for your help, wonderful humor, encouragement, and patience.

The beautiful photograph on the front cover was taken by Madelaine Stanley. Thank you Madelaine, I love it! Madelaine is an 18-year-old senior at Chantilly High School and an aspiring nature photographer. With friends, she spends her free time exploring Washington, D.C., and the surrounding areas. In the future she hopes to see herself working for National Geographic, traversing the world and capturing its sublime wonder in her photographs.

Opalescent Beauty

Admiring from afar, smiling sweetly,
Daughters and grandchildren are her jewels,
Honing their values completely.

Whose brilliance shines in equality,
Her sapphires, garnets, and diamonds,
Of different cuts, exude originality.

Careful manners and demands,
Each fashioned with utmost care,
Guiding words and the steadiest of hands.

Knowing not the power of her beauty,
Or her reserved way with words,
Poise and grace mark writing creativity.

For all her wisdom, she has on loan,
Qualities of the highest standard,
A wiser woman I have never known.

Embarking to speak from her inner voice,
Finishing out her many chapters,
The subject is whim to Fancy's choice.

In loving appreciation,
Your Granddaughter,
Angela

I. Love, Friendship and Family

Heartbreak

❖❖❖

Curse, cry — languish — wait —
Love left me behind.
I bemoaned my fate,
Being young and blind.

Then a dear old aunt of mine,
Compassionate, and serious,
Said regrets are out of line.
She told me this, and told me thus —

"Be happy, darling, and be gay.
Don't give your foolish heart away.
Never, never sit and pout,
Wear your dancing slippers out.
There are plenty of fish in yonder lake."
And quickly I did land one!
I relinquished my heart, and it did break —
Now sorrow's my companion.

The Follies of Youth
❖❖❖

Love's stealth caught me by surprise.
Blinded by my lover's sighs,
I stole from my Arcadian vale,
Where faith, hope, and charity prevail.

High on Wings of Love we sped,
Following where fancy led,
Living on love, frolic, and thrills,
Dreaming of El Dorado's hills.

We built lofty towers in Spain,
Where love and joy and beauty reign,
Towers that reached the firmament,
Until joy became discontent.

When the embers of our love were dead,
To my Arcadian home I fled,
Where faith, hope, and charity live on,
But the innocence of youth is gone.

How much more will I have to pay
For fiddling precious life away?
I know, from the wisdom granted me,
That charity is not always free.

Did I not stand by my window last night
And see, outside, by the moon's hazy light,
   Folly's ghosts looming in the air,
   And the old piper waiting there?

   All my courage I must gather,
   Although I would really rather
   Relive the follies of my youth
Than face the mirage-lifted truth.

Love's Traitor

❖❖❖

Nothing's as sweet as a secret romance,
Until you are faced with doubts;
Then you sigh for reassurance
Or resort to jealous pouts,
For that euphoric rapture
That every lover knows.
Doubt is love's traitor
And grief is what it shows.

The Concept of Love
❖❖❖

When I adopted Anna Lee,
It was obvious as could be
That each of my other three
Were consumed with jealousy.
(Oh, for an olive branch or dove!)

Gathering candles, my children round me came,
And were given one, lit by the mother flame.
(Stilling the green-eyed monster was my aim.)
Comparing the flame to mother love,
Was an inspiration from above!

They noticed how each flame
Was exactly the same,
And with wide-open eyes,
Each one could visualize
The concept of love.

Yet, when Christmas came
They forgot the flame,
Becoming little calculators,
Tallying up their gifts and favors —
Push had come to shove!

A Love Story
❖❖❖

There once was this couple,
Or so I have been told,
Who remained good friends,
Though their romance grew cold.

The lady vacationed in Greece
With some of her friends,
This is how the story begins, and
This is how it ends:

Pictures that they took
Were placed on Facebook.
The young man saw her picture there,
The girl with the flaming red hair!

He was ever gallant and bold,
And so he called his friend of old,
And asked if he could meet somewhere,
That girl with the gorgeous red hair.

She liked what she heard about him,
But all the same,
He had at one time been
Her friend's old flame.

It was a surprise when he called
Out of the blue,
And she answered the phone
Before she knew.

Melissa liked talking to Matthew, so
He called when he had a chance,
And this was the beginning
Of a long distance romance.

She lived in one state,
And he in another,
So they had to make plans
For meeting each other.

They met in proud Charleston,
That southern town by the sea,
And later they decided
That's where their wedding would be.

In the end, I was blessed with
A new grandson,
And they now have
a little one!

When I Was Feeling Down
❖❖❖

When I was feeling down,
I donned a pretty gown
With ruffles to caress my throat,
And thumbed through poetry of note.

Then into the fire, I did stare,
Rocking in my favorite chair,
Vanquishing the way of tears —
All the hurts of yesteryears.

I began to rock and rock,
Rising when I heard a knock —
My great grandsons came trooping in,
Each, with a mischievous grin.

"Tell about the olden days," they say,
And all my sadness was washed away.
We talked about all kinds of things —
Wild strawberries and grapevine swings!

We discussed Biblical stories like Noah's ark,
And Jonah in the belly of a whale or shark;
About Elijah's cave on Mt. Carmel,
In the days of Ahab and Jezebel.

How Elijah could raise the dead
And bring down fire from overhead.
How he departed in a chariot of fire
And ascended into paradise or higher!

As the evening quickly wore on,
We discussed ancestors long gone.
Children love to hear stories of old,
Or at least, that is what I've been told.

The hour was late, when I heard the clock chime
And I saw it was way past their bedtime.
As they were leaving, the boys said,
"Say your prayers and go to bed."

Her Letter

❖❖❖

At the time, he could hardly believe
That his love had gone like that –
They moved away when her mother
Married an aristocrat.

The mailman handed him her letter
On the way to his boat,
He is puzzling over it,
For this is what she wrote:

I have only a minute or two
To write this little missive to you.
I'm on my way to the Autumn Ball,
(Where my mother has bedecked the hall),
Wearing jewels beyond compare,
With a tiara in my hair,
And, Ray, I know you would simply love my gown –
It's from the most exclusive boutique in town.

Why am I thinking of you today,
When you are thousands of miles away?
I've been seeing Bill Barton's son –
He will go far they say,
So how can I tell everyone
That I'm smitten with Ray?

Ah, Ray, do you remember when
I promised to wait for you?
I was only seventeen,
And you had turned twenty-two.
You called me your honey,
Even though I love to dance and flirt,
And you told me if I waited
I would be yours when you struck pay dirt.

All I have ever wanted, Ray —
Wanted all my life,
Is to live on Fisherman's Bay,
And to be your wife.
Of course, money and riches are grand,
So is walking barefoot on the sand!

I will have to close in haste,
I have no more time to waste!
My date is on the stair —
I left him waiting there.

The Red Shirt
(Aviation Ordnanceman)

❖❖❖

My son-in-law is a man among men,
He started working at the age of ten.
In the summer he worked from dusk till dawn,
Tending pigs on the farm he worked upon,
Sometimes helping the mamas give birth
Or helping the farmer plow the earth.

Growing up in Lancaster, PA,
He always dreamed of getting away.
He joined the navy at seventeen,
To see the sights he had never seen.
In '66, went through Boot Camp at Great Lakes,
Showing the Navy that he had what it takes.

Proudly wearing a red shirt with a flaming "piss-pot,"
Loading 2,000-lb bombs on planes for their cat shot.
Drinking coffee laced with JP-5,
Kicked those Ordies into overdrive!
If You Ain't Ordnance You Ain't Sh.., he'd say,
Bombs are coming up from the Hanger Bay!

From seaman recruit, as an ordnance handler,
Advancing through the ranks to a full commander!
Retiring after serving his country for thirty-five years,
On to SAIC to support Tom-a-Hawk for a few years.

Since the Pentagon was still under construction
From 9-11 and Al-Qaeda's terrorist destruction,
It was off to Crystal City he decided to go –
A new government job working for the CNO!

Terry worked with pigs at the age of ten
And he is back working with pigs again –
The pigs are precision strike weapons now,
They are the Flying Pigs of JSOW!

An Accolade to My Sister, Lee

❖❖❖

Steeped in solitude, I write this loving accolade
To a sister, whose inward beauty shall never fade!
Her name is Leoma, but we call her Lee,
And she is one of the best in our family.
When you need someone to listen, someone to care,
You can depend on her! She will always be there!

She can dance the Charleston, and the Wiggle Toe,
And she is always busy and on the go.
She loves travel, music, and art,
And when she gives, it's from the heart.
She is witty, and bright, and always a lady,
And she looks damn fine for a gal just turned eighty.

Echoes of the Past
❖❖❖

Echoes of the past haunt me now and then,
Echoes louder than thunder,
That tear my heart asunder.
Echoes of the past are haunting me again!

I'm drowning in the sea
Of a happy memory,
Feeling so lonely,
It heightens the pain,
And resembles joy only,
As tears resemble rain.

It was I, who chose to walk away,
Oh, so heartbroken and sad —
I'd give anything for yesterday
And all the dreams we had.

How can I forget the past,
And let my heart soar free?
"By giving up dreams so vast,"
The echoes answer me.

The Fool

The fool looked me straight in the eye,
Promising a sweet tomorrow —
And crossed his heart and hoped to die.
An even bigger fool am I,
If I ask for pain and sorrow.

Other promises were not kept,
Leaving me sad and forsaken,
I wept as I had never wept,
And night had gone before I slept:
Oh, it's sunny now I waken!

Jealousy nipped the bud too soon,
And let our romance go awry.
I slept away each day till noon,
To wake beneath a winter moon:
At last — at last — no tears to cry!

Once more to laugh, once more to sing,
To pet the dog, and tease the cat,
To forget about everything;
Finding hope in an early spring
And learning to give tit for tat!

Love's Sad Song
❖❖❖

I put my first love on a pedestal,
Until he had a fall,
And found solace in
Women and alcohol.

My next loves were like him,
Other than their looks,
That's why I buried myself
In my romance books.

None are so blind
As those who cannot see,
So I've given up crying woe
To live vicariously.

The Man I Love and the Man Who Loves Me
❖❖❖

The man who loves me,
I can clearly see,
Is a fine upstanding gentleman,
A man of solid worth.
The man I love is a wandering man,
A gypsy since his birth.

He tells adventurous tales of China,
Sojourning near the sea,
And Scotland where the Queen
Invited him to tea.

The man I love has many
A fine tale to tell.
The man who loves me is staid,
And boring as hell!

Sometimes I really think
Love is just a curse;
Hurting the man who loves me
May be even worse!

Change of Heart
❖❖❖

This I say, and have said before,
I'm through with love forevermore!
Let other fools moan and cry,
When their lovers say good-bye.
I'm not one to sit and sigh
Over love — and that's no lie.

I met a new man the other day,
And he's interesting in his way.
Perhaps I'll try to catch his eye.
About my vow, who cares? Not I.
A change of heart, I'm positive,
Is a woman's prerogative!

Champagne Wishes
❖❖❖

Champagne wishes
And fantasy dreams,
Happy with — or
Without me it seems.

You'd keep me safe
On an island somewhere,
And visit —
When you had time to spare.

Always longing —
Longing for what?
You are adventurous
And I am not.

Another fancy?
Gamble — replace —
The older with
A newer face?

I — here —
And you — where?
Oceans to swim
If you care.

Rumors
❖❖❖

With head held high, midst whispers false or true,
She did not weep, and her face held no frown.
Shadows smoldered deep in those eyes of brown,
Giving credence to gossip, rumors flew –

Loving her valiant soul, beauty, and grace,
Her husband then – his face a thundercloud,
Believed in her innocence – clear and loud –
For sorrow's toll was written on her face.

Murmuring low, she told him how love had fled –
That she had looked for him by plane and car
While he hid in space, above moon and star –
Thus, she did go, and that is all she said.

Jean Boggs Baker

For My Grandson
❖❖❖

Your warm heart — so loving and giving —
Valiant spirit and zest for living,
Make you a Grandson to be celebrated!
You fill my life with joy — I am elated,
And hope your birthday dreams come true,
Even though you may have a slew.

The Red Hat Society

In anticipation,
Faces aglow,
Arrayed in purple and
A red chapeau.
Playing dress-up
For an afternoon tea —
Partying with
The Red Hat Society!

Ladies in their Red Hats,
Greeting everyone,
Gathering for friendship and nurturing,
Gathering for fun!

Making friends with time,
Finding autumn is delight,
Freed from responsibility
Without feeling so uptight;
Coming to realize
The setting sun,
Is more exquisite than
The rising one!

A Stricken Heart
❖❖❖

She stood before the church of her childhood,
And after staring for a span,
Said, "I shall never at your altar stand
And exchange vows with any man."

Her heart was filled with despair,
She bit back a bitter sigh —
There, railing against a faithless love,
Howled her anguish to the sky.

It was with a stricken heart,
She bid her love adieu.
She believed the whispering tongues,
Until they proved untrue.

She listens to that lonesome whistle,
As it echoes down the track,
When he left he took her heart,
And he never gave it back.

Their love is gone forever,
And will forever go unblessed,
Though she settled for another,
Grief weighs heavy upon her breast.

God's Love
❖❖❖

The night is cold and gloomy,
Moon-shadows drape the wall.
The might of God protects me,
I'm not afraid at all.
I am not afraid even though
The night sounds are creepy,
And I sense a presence below.
Do I hear quiet footsteps?
The stairs creak, one by one,
And God's love surrounds me
Like the rays of the sun.

My Mother

❖❖❖

Hers, the hands that tended us,
With such cheerful tenderness;
And when she'd hear the baby cry,
Softly, she'd sing a lullaby.

Baked our bread and sewed our dresses,
Washed our faces and combed tresses;
Plucked bouquets from beds of loam,
Making bare existence — home.

My Dad
❖❖❖

Up before the crack of dawn,
Puts the horse's harness on —
Off to High Field he has gone.

Cleared new ground for his cornfield,
(Aches and pains he concealed),
Hoping for a better yield.

In new ground how crops do grow,
Again it's time to plow and hoe,
Before the meadow he can mow.

Rings to go in each shoat's snout!
Shoats will root potatoes out
Before they begin to sprout.

Fences to mend, horses to shoe,
Find time to clean the chimney flue.
A farmer's work is never through!

It seems a farmer can never win,
Do the same work again and again,
Until time to bring the harvest in.

Jean Boggs Baker

The Varsity Coach
❖❖❖

He won his first bowling trophy at age eight,
It was taller than he — he thought that was great!
In bowling his high series was eight-thirty-one,
All strikes except three in the three games that he won.

Winning a bowling tournament when he was in high school,
He was invited to Tel-Aviv — he thought that was cool,
Was asked to bowl in the Maccabi Games;
(An important Jewish style Olympic event);
Because he scored strikes in so many frames;
But instead — to high school graduation he went.

Won a scholarship to U. of Charleston, in baseball;
He loves sports, plays them exceedingly well, plays them all;
Continued to bowl while at the University,
Graduating with honors and a teaching degree.

He teaches Phys Ed in Rochester, NY,
And is a varsity coach at Brighton High;
Lately inducted into the Jewish Hall of Fame —
My grandson-in-law: Jason Wasserman is his name!

Coal Mining

❖❖❖

Our coal mining heritage –
Conserved by men of courage
Courting death in a daunting gloom
To fuel this land and make it boom.

They plunge into the earth below
And tunnel where they need to go,
Looking for black gold — cached sunshine,
Another vein of coal to mine.

Millions of tons of coal are found
Miles from sunlight, deep underground.
And cap lamps on helmets widely fling
Their bright shining lights where Coal is King.

Roofs may collapse, and earth may quiver,
Or water seep in like a river —
An engineer deals with cave-in and flood,
Drexel's up for the challenge, it's in his blood!

Mining is dark, dirty work —
Carelessness, and — dangers lurk!
In subterranean depths, day after day,
Hardship for triumph is the price they pay.

My Grandson's New Wife
❖❖❖

My grandson took a new wife,
And she's the love of his life.
A blended family, they've created —
With her little girl, and his little boy, and
Their own little one — they are elated!

She's a lovely young woman,
And she's a great mommy, too!
She has high hopes, and lots of
Interesting things to do.

She loves all kinds of music,
From country to rock;
Her favorite band is
"New Kids on the Block."

A stay at home mom,
She has chosen to be,
But later plans to
Get her nursing degree.

A Great Man

The chill of age is on him,
Frost is coating what's left of his hair,
Once so vigorous and vim,
Now he nods by the fire in his chair.

He was a great man of majestic mien
Throughout those turbulent days,
Whose heroic feats often went unseen,
Though many still sing his praise.

His exploits he dim-remembers,
And his dreams are beginning to fade,
Like a wild fire's dying embers
When lightning strikes in a bosky glade.

Some of his doctors, in their discussions,
Say cobwebs are tangling his brain –
It's the residue of old concussions –
But I've never heard him complain!

II. Childhood and Youth

Chase

❖❖❖

Where's that little towhead
With the impish grin?
Is he thinking up some mischief, or
On that swing again?

There's no one like Chase,
He's utter delight.
The problem is
He's in love with height.

When he swings,
He likes to swing high,
He has this urge
To embrace the sky.

The last time he was on a swing,
Flying so high, and flying fast,
He jumped toward the open sky,
Now his ankle is in a cast.

Karly
❖❖❖

A lovely girl
silky brown hair
tresses to curl
a charming air
a dimpled chin
a twinkle in
those big blue eyes
like evening skies
a bit daring
very caring
loves to pose
try new clothes
gems and bows
sings with glee
for you and me
she's only three
a dance, a whirl
a happy girl

Lacey

❖❖❖

Happy dreams, little one,
Your life has just begun.
Nothing's as endearing and as good
As the blossoming of babyhood.

Lacey's a darling when I hold her,
Slumbering softly on my shoulder.
She's resting her precious little head
Till her mother tucks her into bed.

Hugs and Kisses

❖❖❖

Money was scarce and I
Was feeling low enough to cry,
When my daughter handed me a gift
Wrapped and adorned with my best tie.

After I opened my present and found
Games of tic-tac-toe inside,
I scolded her for ruining my necktie
In the big bow she had tied.

She didn't get upset with me,
She gave me a hug instead,
Then she looked up at me,
And this is what she said:

"I filled this box with hugs and kisses,
I hoped they'd make you glad,
I wish it could've been a million dollars,
Because I love you, Dad!"

Her symbols for a kiss and a hug,
To me, were a cross and a naught.
I apologized profusely and told her
That I had been feeling distraught.

"Daddy, don't apologize,
We don't have any money, I know.
I heard Mommy say you were feeling bad
Because business is terribly slow."
Then, with a melancholy sigh,
"I didn't find any ribbon,
That's why I used your pretty tie."

It has been many years
Since my books were in the red,
Still I fondly remember
What my little daughter said.

Olivia

Though she is a tiny lass,
No bigger than a minute,
She has stolen my heart —
With everything that's in it.

A delightful blue eyed, jovial child,
Short blonde hair, no sign of curls.
Above dimpled chin, a joyful smile,
Shows her two wee sparkling pearls.

The smile of bliss upon her face
Proves that her world's a happy place.
May life's marvels never cease,
And her happiness increase!

Trace
❖❖❖

In a swimming pool, on a bright summer day,
A son, being tossed in the air, flips right in,
Then swims back to his dad to be tossed again.
He's practicing for the Olympics today.

And, oh! What a time of solid bliss,
When his mom comes out to play like this!
He laughed for the joy of being alive,
And showed her how well he could swim and dive.

Hold on to those moments as long as you can,
Your little fledgling is readying his wings
For the Olympics, among other things,
And before you know it he will be a man!

Trent's Song

❖❖❖

What dreams do you hold
In those big brown eyes?
Are you a sky walker
Patrolling the skies?
Will you wield your light saber
To slay Darth Vader,
And other villains in the sky?

When you lasso a cloud to
Take a little ride,
Are the Jedi warriors
Waiting by your side?
Do you sing a secret song?
Do the warriors sing along,
As you go gliding through the sky?

You'll see wonder upon wonder,
Streak of lightning, clap of thunder;
Gather rainbows — roll them up;
Drink your fill from wonder's cup.
Hurry home when night is nigh,
Bring enchantment from the sky —
And Mama will sing you a lullaby.

Playing Ball
❖❖❖

It's baseball season again!
When you play ball,
Do you try your best to win?

When you bat the ball,
Do you make it soar?
Do you run like the wind
To hear the crowd roar?

When you pitch the ball,
Do you strike someone out?
Do you sometimes throw a curve
And listen to them shout?

Are you a good loser
When you're playing sports,
Or do you get angry
And feel out of sorts?

When you've been playing ball
And the other team has won,
Remember it's just a game,
And you are playing for fun.

Bowling Baby
❖❖❖

My son loves bowling,
He takes after me;
Whatever daddy does,
He is sure to see.

He watches bowling videos
On such and such a day;
Though he mimics each bowler,
His idol's Walter Ray.

Since he loves bowling so,
We entered him in a league.
He is barely three,
But he thinks he's very big!

His ball rolled in the gutter
When he fell and bumped his knee.
His mother kisses the pain away,
So I knew it was up to me.

"Still hurts! Try again!"
Was his plaintive call,
Was it the pain in his knee,
Or the channel ball?

The Rose
❖❖❖

In the early morning light,
I did chance to see,
Dressed in nightgown lily white,
Our child who's nearly three.
Hesitant, standing in bare feet,
Overwhelmed by fragrance so sweet —
Then she buried her nose
In petals laced with dew —
A rose, a white-white rose,
The one she chose for you!

My Great Grandson
(Based on a True Story)
❖❖❖

Alex knew much about our presidents
Before he was nine,
He knew who came first and,
Who was next in line:

<u>18th Century</u>

First, came the august Washington,
That great courageous truthful one.

Second, the senior Adams won,
A wise man and an honest one.

<u>19th Century</u>

And our third was the great Jefferson.
He acquired the Louisiana Territory
From the Bonaparte, Napoleon.

Our fourth was James Madison,
"Father of the Constitution."

Then James Monroe, our fifth, won —
Known for the "Monroe Doctrine."

Our sixth was President Adams' son,
   Recognized as "the eloquent one."

Seventh, Andrew Jackson, is here,
   Nicknamed "Old Hickory,"
   From the American frontier.

Van Buren, our eighth, was the first one,
   Born an American citizen.

Our ninth, William Henry Harrison,
   Died in office soon after he won.

The first to succeed a president in,
Was Vice President Tyler, number ten.

Eleventh, Polk, was a "dark horse,"
   He favored expansion, of course.

Taylor came in twelfth, you know.
"Old Rough and Ready" was a hero,
   In our war with Mexico.

Fillmore, thirteenth, filled Taylor's space,
With no vice president in place.

Then Pierce, fourteenth, governs the nation.
At the end of his administration,
Pierce was denied re-nomination.

James Buchanan, fifteenth, won the race,
A northerner with southern sympathies,
Was at that time known as a "doughface."

"Honest Abe," sixteenth, ruled our land.
And the country forced Lincoln's hand.

When Abraham Lincoln was shot,
Johnson, seventeenth, filled the slot.
First president to be impeached, you'll note,
Acquitted in the Senate by one vote.

Eighteenth, Grant, was elected twice, what's more,
Grant was a hero of the Civil War.

Nineteenth, Hayes, was elected
And our esteem protected.

Garfield, our twentieth, was somewhat skilled
In restoring prestige to
The presidency before he was killed.

Our twenty-first, Arthur, his office filled.
Arthur was widely distrusted, in fact,
Until he passed the Civil Service Act.

Cleveland, twenty-second, was selected.
After the Civil War,
He was the first Democrat elected.

Our twenty-third, Benjamin Harrison, won.
He was William Henry Harrison's grandson.

Twenty-fourth, Cleveland, is back again!
The only president to leave the White House,
Then four years later he walked back in.

Twice, McKinley, twenty-fifth, was in.
He was forced into the Spanish American war,
That took ninety days for us to win.

20th Century

After McKinley's assassination,
Twenty-sixth, Roosevelt, leads our nation.
He won the Nobel Peace Prize for his
Russo-Japanese War mediation.

Taft, twenty-seventh, won on Election Day.
He was a progressive and
They said that old "Teddy" had "cut enough hay."

Then Wilson, number twenty-eight, —
Held in his hands our nation's fate.

Harding came in number twenty-nine,
And was given the first
U.S. Child Welfare Program to sign.

Thirtieth, Coolidge was next in line.
His active inactivity seemed to suit the mood
And certain needs of the country fine.

The Great Depression we underwent —
Hoover, thirty-first, was president.

Thirty-second, FDR, dealt with the condition.
And he went on to break the "no third term" tradition.

Thirty-third, Truman, with some aplomb,
Ended World War II with the A-bomb.

Our thirty-fourth was — man of the hour —
General Dwight D. Eisenhower.

Our thirty-fifth, Kennedy, was shot,
Before he had time to do a lot.
We were on the brink of nuclear war
Soon after "The Bay of Pigs" fiasco,
Trying to overthrow Fidel Castro.

Thirty-sixth, Lyndon Johnson, filled the spot,
And will be best known by the fact
That he signed the Civil Rights Act.

Thirty-seventh, Nixon, resigned
Rather than face impeachment for
Trying to divert investigation
Of the so-called "Watergate"
Scandal during his administration.

Thirty-eighth, Ford, was the man in line,
When Richard Nixon had to resign.

Then Carter was number thirty-nine.
The energy crisis and inflation
Overwhelmed Carter's administration,
As well as, hostages in Iran
And the war waged in Afghanistan.

Fortieth, an actor of some fame,
Of course, Ronald Reagan was his name.

Forty-first, Bush, will be noted for
"Operation Just Cause" in the Panama
Invasion; and the Persian Gulf War.

Clinton, forty-second, had problems to face,
Was impeached for a scandal and faced disgrace.

21Century

Forty-third, the younger Bush will be best known for
Homeland Security and the Iraqi War.

Forty-fourth, Obama, wins the race.
The only African American President
  Elected in the United States.

Alex knew all kinds of trivia
  About their lives,
And could even tell you the
  Names of their wives.

I asked who was president when I was born,
  And thought I'd stump him here,
But he told me Calvin Coolidge,
  When I gave him the year.

I told Alex he could be president some day,
  He just looked at me then said, "Not!"
When I asked why, he said,
  "I'd be afraid that I'd be shot."

Trent

❖❖❖

Trent is an outgoing, sunshiny boy
Whose life overflows with laughter and joy.
Filled with vitality, his spirit zings,
And he is sweet-natured about most things.

Pretend and make-believe are
Some games that he's played,
When he dressed up in costumes
That his mother made.

He wears Batman pajamas
And slippers on his feet,
And he thinks a Batman video
Will make his life complete.

Asking for a Batman video game to play,
Trent urged, "Let's go shopping for it today."
Dad and Mom shook their heads no. He said, "Okay,
I can wait till that rabbit holiday!"

Wednesday's Child
❖❖❖

Born a Wednesday's child,
To face a life of woe —
"You can flip the coin,"
My mother told me so.

She helped me thrust away my tears,
How fortunate for me,
The flip side of woe
Is total jubilee!

III. POEMS BASED ON TRUE STORIES

The Sheriff's Wife

❖❖❖

A feisty little old lady named Lou
Was in a snit! She was going to sue!
Her husband, the sheriff, would rue the day,
He was to blame! She would make him pay!
On a rainy night, they had a wreck,
And she came close to breaking her neck.

All during the cold winter rains,
She sat nursing her aches and pains.
While her husband was out chasing crooks,
He left her at home to read her books.

This feisty little lady named Lou
Wouldn't be treated like an old shoe.
After more than fifty years of wedded bliss,
She'd take her chances on becoming a Miss.

The insurance man asked if she planned to sue,
So she said, "You bet! I am entitled to."
Egged on by lawyers, she took a stand,
And settled for more than sixty grand!

A Set of Blue Willow

Like yesterday, I remember,
More than seventy long years ago,
The early dewy morning, when
Dressed in riding skirt, my mother
Rode on horseback to Elana,
Over the hill to Hamrick's store.

On a skittish horse she rode there,
For a set of new blue willow,
Put them in flour for safe-keeping,
Packed her beautiful new dishes,
That the grocer loaded for her.
On the nervous horse he placed them,
Securing them with her saddle.

On the way home, Tony saw it,
Just a piece of plain white paper,
The horse reared straight up on hind legs,
Broke the girth where dad had tied it.
On the dirt road fell the saddle,
Fell the dishes and my mother.

The mail carrier saw it happen,
Saw my bruised and dusty mother,
Caught the horse and fixed the saddle,
Tied the girth with her shoelaces,
Made fast the flour sacks behind her.

When my mom unpacked her china,
Every piece was chipped or broken,
Gone, her beautiful blue willow —
The blue willow like her mother's,
Gone, a year of scrimp and scraping!

Wedding in Old Charleston
❖❖❖

In the elegance of old Charleston,
Two families gathered round,
For a taste of romance,
In that southern coastal town.

The bride and groom came strolling
A lover's lane, hand in hand.
The day was rare and wondrous
For the wedding they had planned.

Saying their vows to one another,
In a gazebo smart and trim;
Wearing God's collar,
The groom's brother married them.

We toasted bride and groom
With some sparkling champagne,
Then walked down lover's lane,
Across a bridge in the beautiful park,
And under a sprawling old oak tree,
Captured the moment for posterity.

The reception was a grand affair,
Good friends mingled with the family there.
Then they were off for some honeymoon fun,
Renewing the spirits of everyone.

Grandpa Lost

❖❖❖

While hanging clothes on the line,
I heard my baby crying.
The sound was coming from across the street,
I thought my ears were lying.

A little boy was holding her,
He may have been eleven,
She was fighting him, and
Screaming to high heaven.

I scooped her up and thanked him
For keeping her from the street,
I held her but I was shaking,
From my head down to my feet.

"Grandpa lost!" She cried.
They had gone to the grocery store,
And she walked home.
It was at least six blocks, or more.

She was just a little tyke,
Still in diapers, not quite two.
"You crossed all those busy streets;"
And you are sopping wet, too!"

"Big cars stopped," she said.
Was it the traffic light?
We were just lucky that she
Timed it precisely right.

When we walked in the house, her Grandma said,
"Thank God! You found her and she's back!"
She got off the phone, saying, "I thought
Grandpa would have a heart attack."

When My Dad Was Young
❖❖❖

On a cold and snowy December day,
Cattle bawled and the horses neighed —
As snow was flying all around,
From the open door of an old barn loft,
My Dad was pitching fodder down.
He stepped on one loose board
And it flung him out to the ground;
Landing on the point of a cut cornstalk,
It stabbed beneath his chin,
Through his neck into his mouth,
That sharp cornstalk went in.

When blood began gushing out in spurts,
Dad pressed his thumb tight against the hurt,
Slowing the bleeding — helping the pain —
Grateful it wasn't his jugular vein.
The wound was severe he couldn't drink,
And he ached so he could hardly think.
He knew that he would have to have it checked,
When water ran out the hole in his neck.

He needed stitches — Mom told him so —
Whether or not he wanted to go!
His Uncle Andrew — a surgeon of note —
Gave him a shot and stitched up his throat!

An Imaginary Friend
❖❖❖

When my daughter was little
and playing alone,
I noticed her talking
on her telephone.
She called her friend Bessie,
now, who could that be?
No one that I knew,
and neither did she.

She asked me if Bessie
could come by to play.
I wondered about it a moment,
then told her okay.
When she was lonely,
Bessie would come by that day.

Before I knew it,
Bessie had moved in to stay.
Bessie was a playmate
that I couldn't see,
but she kept Gail happy,
and that worked for me.

At mealtime I had to
set her a plate.
Thank goodness, pretend food was
all that she ate.
I had to be careful where
I sat down.
"Don't sit on Bessie," she would say,
with a frown.

Once she had to go to the bathroom
in the middle of the night,
I told her to take Bessie,
and she simply said, "All right."
Bessie was with us until the baby
was old enough to play,
then it seems her friend,
Bessie, just left one day.

An Intruder

❖❖❖

It's that time of year again —
Last minute shopping to do —
Dinner dishes were stacked in the sink,
And off to the mall we flew.

When we got home,
We were all tuckered out,
It had been a long day
Before our shopping bout.

Putting down our shopping bags,
Gail, Lori, and I went to bed,
But my teenage daughter
Chose to polish her nails instead.

Donna, waiting for her nails to dry,
Sat down and turned out the light.
She wanted to rest her eyes, and
The lamp seemed awfully bright.

She woke with a start when she heard
The lock on the back door click
And she sat there frozen,
When the door opened so quick.

She flipped on the light
And barely got out a squeak,
Before he was gone
And she was able to speak.

Gail jumped out of bed,
Stumbling over a baseball bat
Placed there for protection
And was out the door — just like that!

He was long gone, but
She found our keys in the door
Where we had left them,
When we came back from the store.

Lori, my three-year-old granddaughter,
Her eyes wide with wonder bright,
Wanted to know what was happening
In the middle of the night.

I called the sheriff's office,
And he asked, "When and where?"
Before I could explain further,
He said, "I'll be right there."

I rinse off the dirty dishes,
Put them in a pan
And hide them in the oven
As quick as I can.

When we explained things to the Sheriff,
He said, "We can't track him down."
It's been raining and
No finger prints can be found.

He noticed Lori, dying for his attention, and
Started to ask about her Christmas wishes,
But she opened the oven door, and beaming,
Said, "This is where we keep our dirty dishes!"

Winter Flood
❖❖❖

After a flood one winter morning,
Down the muddy road I scurried
To catch the little school bus,
(A covered truck with benches).

Rode the bus five miles to Nebo,
To the new school I attended.
Had to cross the creek by foot log,
Cross that muddy, swollen deluge,
Where waters rose, and waters surged.

Across the foot log I started —
(Each school day I crossed it,
Crossed the creek where water trickled.)
Halfway across, I faltered,
Looked into the seething waters,
Saw that swirling, howling tide,
Tossing trash that it had gathered.

Was the foot log moving 'neath me?
Moving down stream with the waters —
Swaying dizzily, I lost my footing,
Fell into those freezing waters!

My older cousin, Lula, saw me,
Saw the current sucking me under;
Jumped into that cold muddy torrent,
Into its trash tossed turbulence;
Pulled me from the rushing waters.

When our teacher saw us,
Saw us drenched and dripping,
Had us stand near the coal stove,
(The pot-bellied coal stove,
In the middle of the classroom).
Told us to take off our stockings.

Lula peeled off her stockings,
But I was wearing long johns,
The underwear that I hated,
That Mom made me wear in winter.
(I knew the kids would snicker.)

Since I wouldn't remove my stockings,
School was dismissed that morning —
Like the little first grade children,
I was helped across the foot log,
Across that muddy swirling current,
Where our school bus was waiting.

When I reached home, I was freezing,
And my teeth were chattering.
Took a hot bath in a wash tub,
(We had no indoor plumbing).
Drank hot cocoa that Mom made me,
Then my dolls she gave me, and
Put me to bed like a baby.

Sitting With Trace
(My great grandson)

On his way back from the Temple of Doom,
Indiana Jones comes into the room,
Dressed all in khaki, wearing a Sam Browne belt,
Jacket of leather, and fedora of felt;
Cracking a ten-foot bullwhip that can't be beat,
But where are the boots that he wears on his feet?
I suppose he left them at the door,
So he wouldn't scuff his mother's floor.

Home again, from the land of make-believe,
Trace bounds out the door with his chocolate lab,
And throws a ball for his dog to retrieve.
I make him dinner and he eats just a dab,
Then he's engrossed in a video game.
Alternate reality all the same —

At bedtime he dawdles as long as he dares,
When I fuss and complain that he's too slow —
"Patience is a virtue!" or so he declares.
I say, "Tomorrow's a school day, you know!"
After prayers are said, and he's tucked in bed,
I ask God to bless every hair on his head.

My Uncle Clay

This tale is about my Uncle Clay,
Who had been butchering beeves all day.
He whistled up his horse, at day's close,
And started home with blood on his clothes.

Twilight was fast approaching night,
Clay looked neither to left nor right.
Up that lonely back road, horse with rider trots,
Visions of hot food and rest, among Clay's thoughts.

An old bobcat, beginning to doze,
Smelled that fresh blood on the rider's clothes.
The cat leaped on the back of the horse,
Frightening the horse and Clay, of course.

The bucking horse and Clay began to fight,
When suddenly a car lit up the night;
A Model T, with its bright lights on.
With an angry screech, that cat was gone!

Once the horse was fed and in the barn,
And he had a chance to tell his yarn,
My Uncle Clay swore by the point of his knife
That he'd never had such a scare in his life.

Labor Day Weekend of '54
❖❖❖

Working for the FBI in '54, and
Home for Labor Day weekend —
The foggy morning hadn't blinked before
He was off to meet a friend.

In that sharp curve below Bradley Field,
A car swerved toward him coming fast —
Forcing my brother off the road —
He slid on loose gravel when it passed.

Skidding into the hillside knocked him across
The road, causing a loss of control;
His head splintered the windshield when
He slammed into a telephone pole.

It left him so stunned and shaken that
Before any gas he could give her,
The truck rolled over a fifty foot bank
And plunged into the big Elk River.

He kicked out the jagged windshield glass,
Climbing out into that muddy river's roar —
He garnered all his strength and with
A burst of energy, Alan swam to shore.

Whether it was fate or just plain good luck,
He managed to somehow or other,
Climb that steep fifty foot bank,
And hitched a ride with his friend's brother.

The Northern Lights (Aurora Borealis)
❖❖❖

My family was outside
One chilly autumn at twilight,
When the sky opened wide,
Down-pouring vivid streams of light.
Spectacular beauty filled the night —
Billowing sheets of mystical light!
We gazed in awe and wonder at the bright array
Of radiant celestial colors on display.

Aurora Borealis — despite her charm —
In the early days, could frighten and alarm.
It seemed as though the sky would try
and part to show a further sky,
and then a further — and the three
would bare the brink of eternity!
My poor mother fell to her knees —
The world was coming to an end!
She prayed for mercy and heart's ease —
Rainbow colors danced on the wind!

And then we chanced to hear on the radio —
For a few nights —
How others had been frightened by the show
Of Northern Lights!

Through Wind and Snow
❖❖❖

I will always remember
That cold day in December,
Two feet of snow on the ground
And it was still coming down!

The coffee was just beginning to brew,
As I peeled an apple and cored it, too.
I shivered on the porch, just outside my door,
To throw a deer the peeling and apple core.

I drew back my arm, and just as I threw,
I heard a loud bang, and that's when I knew
I had been locked out by a gust of wind,
Now with snow and ice I'd have to contend!

Me, in my slippers and old flannel nightgown,
With wind whipping and spitting snow all around,
Biting back an expletive under my breath,
And knowing if I stood there I'd freeze to death.

Not waiting for fate, I used my head,
And hurried out to the storage shed.
My toes were numb and I was beginning to sneeze,
When I found some old boots that came up to my knees.

Then I went trudging through the snow
To the old dead Silverado,
And found a survival blanket in the truck door.
Wrapped in Mylar, I wasn't as cold as before!

Down that rough hillside I did go,
Through half a mile of blinding snow,
Then up a mountain through pine trees,
Climbing through snow up to my knees.

So glad to see my sister's house in the distance,
Knowing she would offer coffee and assistance;
Struggling and sweating in wind and cold,
Was enough to kill this eighty-year-old.

Thanking God for finding that blanket and boots;
Laughing, cause I knew I looked like an old coot.
I told my sister what kept me going was fear
That I would die of embarrassment in this gear!

When I had thawed, her husband, came in
And looked at me with a big ol' grin;
But he looked fairly sober before
Saying, "Come on, let's open your door!"

Getting a ladder from our storage shed,
He climbed in a window over my bed;
In a minute my door was opened wide
And I was elated to be inside!

The Dreamer
❖❖❖

In the early morning cold,
Atop a mossy crag, I rest
And marvel at the splendor.
Far below the hillside's crest
The play of light is tender,
Bathing fog banks in its gold.

Wrapped in dreams, I can barely hear
The singletree chains clank and jangle,
As the old man plows at an angle
And his temper flares,
Through the wash of air,
Slapping reins amid the gear.

He will scrimp and scrape, and then
Plant his crops on a hill so high,
It seems the earth will meet the sky;
And he'll never count the cost,
Lest a blade of grass be lost —
Just one among frugal men!

Acres of land where green grass grows,
Then into haystacks it will go —
Cattle can't forage in the snow.
It seems this farmer's child was born
For climbing hills and hoeing corn —
And loving whims that nature shows!

Since I have whiled away the time,
I hustle up the path,
Dreading to hear his wrath,
Knowing he will say such and such,
Like, dreamers don't amount to much —
And I've another slope to climb!

The Accident

❖❖❖

Eight years old — and she could go where she would,
    As long as she stayed in the neighborhood.
    She's zooming down the street on her bike,
        Trying to decide what she would like.

With the sun on her back and the wind in her hair,
    Wild with glee — in the sweet rush of air,
She rides down quiet back streets, pedaling strong,
    When without volition she bursts into song:

    "Oh, curb me not — this day divine,
        Belongs to me — is wholly mine."
    The street and air with her voice is loud,
        As, when sky is clear without a cloud.

Midst rustling palms, and the tall waving pine,
    And the lush lemon tree's radiant shine,
    Azaleas, gardenias, and fragrant rose,
    Enchant the senses — tease eye and nose.

She is so engrossed in composing her song,
She hits a car as she's riding along.
Her Dad sees her staggering across the lawn
And he rushes to see what is going on.

The child hesitated, and then, "I hit a car," she cries.
"Did a car hit you?" He checks her out, and, "No," she replies,
"The car was parked. I was busy singing and hit the car."
Taking her in to her Mother, he chuckled, "That's bizarre!"
And he has to go after her bike and check out the car.

Toppled in the Street

❖❖❖

Two sisters playing
across the street,
Daddy calls,
"It's time to eat."

They see a car,
it's coming slow,
away down the road,
a mile or so.
Gail runs home
lickety-split,
Donna's shoe flies off, and
she retrieves it,
puts on her shoe
and ties it, too.

Before she could get to her feet,
the car toppled her in the street.
She woke to aches and blaring horns,
and heard the other drivers' scorn;
a neighbor holding her tight;
her Dad stripping gears,
and running every red light.

In the emergency room,
the doctor found that she's
bruised, and asphalt's
embedded in her knees.

When I got home from
the beauty salon,
Gail and a friend
met me on the lawn.

Gail said, "Don't worry, Mom!"
Then she said, in a rush,
"Donna was hit by a car!"
And my legs turned to mush.

"Mom, please don't go all emotional,
Dad took her to the hospital."
Inside, I clamped down my fear,
and grabbed a phone hanging near.

St. Vincent's told me she was
released at nine,
and except for some pain,
she'd be just fine.

Her London Experience
❖❖❖

Around a roaring fire,
Three generations sat together,
With apple logs snapping and cracking,
To ward off the early spring weather.

They were discussing Spring Break,
Angela's senior year, and
A fabulous London tour
Her Clay High teachers had planned.

Angela sensed there would be a problem
With her overprotective mother,
She wouldn't even let her go to camp —
But, maybe, with luck and grandmother!

"That will be an experience of a lifetime."
Granny said, and her Mother said, "That's true!"
Then got up and turned to Angela, saying,
"Come on, baby, we have some shopping to do."

As the plane soared through the sky,
Over the ocean deep,
Angela set her mind adrift to dream
And soon was fast asleep,

At the airport she overheard
Her chaperones talking, and heard one mention
That Angela seemed to be getting
All kinds of unsolicited attention.

When they got to the hotel,
Twins carried Angela's bags up five flights of stairs.
There were no elevators and
The other girls had no one to carry theirs.

Everyone could tell she was an American tourist
And seeing London was a treat,
By the pictures she was taking; by her long curly hair;
And by the sneakers on her feet.

She hoped to tour Buckingham Palace, but the Queen was
In residence, and tours were barred;
Instead, she watched the renowned ceremony
That is the Changing of the Guard.

Angela toured the Tower of London
Where the Crown Jewels were seen.
Where ancient stones echoed murky secrets
And prized ravens walked the green.

The Tower of London, a world famous fortress,
Has served as royal palace, prison, armory, and zoo.
Across the way can be seen the Tower Bridge on
The River Thames and you will see an incredible view.

The Beefeater guards were aware and witty.
Quietly, they were told —
"Go to the chapel and
Hear about heads that rolled!"

They went to a famous pub
Where Shakespeare used to drink,
And the maitre d' served Angela
Quicker than you would think.

Her friend couldn't get his attention, so
She gave Angela her plate.
He came almost immediately,
They no longer had to wait.

Then she visited Westminster Abbey,
A reverent and colossal space,
Where royal weddings, coronations, and
Prominent funerals take place.

A procession of British history — Kings,
Queens, statesmen, heroes, and villains are noted here,
And the Poet's Corner honors famous authors such as
Shakespeare, Milton, Chaucer and others we revere.

They stopped at the Hardrock Café —
Saw wax figurines and bought souvenirs.
Angela bought a garnet ring and a sapphire, and
One of the Queen's favorite perfumes here.

She journeyed to Windsor Castle,
Stepping back in time and history.
This impressive Gothic palace
Is steeped in folklore and mystery.

Windsor is the most famous of all English castles.
Antiques and a plethora of paintings can be seen.
Royals have lived here almost a thousand years and
It's today an Official Residence of the Queen.

Then a visit to the circle of ancient Stonehenge,
A place where dreams can be fired,
It's tied to legends of Merlin and King Arthur,
Who knows what may have transpired!

She explored the Roman Baths,
These were built around thermal springs,
Drawing visitors from across the Roman Empire
For healing power the water brings.

The group stopped at a Shakespearean Theatre
To partake of an elaborate Elizabethan feast.
When a pig's head on a platter was brought in, with an
Apple in its mouth; they weren't surprised in the least.

They were entertained by court jesters,
Jugglers, and magic and amazing feats
Of mystery and strength while
Enjoying an abundance of good eats.

From a crowd of five hundred, or so,
Angela was asked if she would assist the strong man.
She checked the chain, making sure links were intact.
He tells the diners he will break the chain, if he can.

He wraps the chain around his body
And when she snaps the lock,
He breaks the chain with his muscles,
In the tick of a clock.

When it was over — five hundred were leaving at once,
Down a deep street — dark and dangerous.
Angela took her chaperone's arm and
They went hurrying to reach the bus.

Home again — and Angela heard a teacher telling
Her mother that they had been leery as could be,
Afraid Angela might be kidnapped by some characters
Who appeared to be full of guile and treachery.

Angela was thrilled with her tour —
Telling her mother that rather than
Having someone kidnap her,
It was she who locked up a strong man!

The Gypsies
❖❖❖

Gypsies came to our farm in the fall of the year
And my mother viewed them with both interest and fear.
They were a wandering, dark-skinned and dark-eyed race,
Traveling in horse drawn caravans from place to place.

They camped in the scale house where
Our cattle were weighed,
Without our permission, that's
Where the Gypsies stayed.

Gypsies will steal your children,
Mom had heard someone say —
So Dad met us after school,
Until they went away.

They dressed in gaudy colors and
Wore big flashy rings,
And the men were horse traders,
Among other things.

Galloping, their big spirited horses' hoofs
Would make the ground ring.
At night, they played sweet music, and we
Listened to them sing.

Two Gypsy women in glittering dresses,
With long flowing skirts,
And their two little boys dressed in
Cotton shorts and shirts,
Walked up to the house one day —
Asked to use our oven and offered
To tell Mom's fortune in pay.

She let them use her oven and
Kneaded dough for making their bread.
She didn't want them to tell her fortune
Or at least that is what she said.

She told them she was married with six children,
That she was getting old
And it was too late to tell her fortune,
It had already been told.

I envied them their travels,
And with my brown eyes and olive skin,
I could have passed for a Gypsy,
I would have fit right in.

IV. Humor and Whimsy

Candles
❖❖❖

Such an exotic party night —
The rooms are bathed in candlelight.
Lori's candles have a fantastic flair
For flaunting their fragrances in the air.
Candles with their mystical light
Enhance the beauty of the night.
When aflame, they dazzle so,
Casting love-spells in their glow.

Party on,
Dance till dawn!
The music enchants, but
O, my friends,
Don't burn your candles
At both ends!

Story Things Get All Mixed Up
❖❖❖

Please, oh, please leave on the light —
It's so dark in here at night!
I never know what to do
When Billy Goat Gruff
Falls over a bluff,
And Turkey Lurky says, "Moo!"
Sleepy Head says, "Hi! Ho!"
"Come on — let's go," said Slow.
Sleeping Beauty jumps over the moon
And Cinderella straddles a broom;
A big old fox comes from his den
And gobbles up Little Red Hen;
Casper creeps under my sheet
And freezes me with his feet;
Rose red and White as Snow
Get pretty scared, you know.
No sunbeams to fill my cup —
Story things get all mixed up.
Daylight is full of cheer,
It's the light that they fear,
I'll try not to cry tonight,
If you will leave on a light.

She's Just an Old Maid
❖❖❖

Like most young girls of a certain age,
When elegant weddings are the rage,
I fashioned myself a well-made plan
Of power and glory through a man.

Like the others I couldn't wait
And rushed headlong to seal my fate,
Then realized much too late,
That it was really up to me,
To be all that I could be,
And recently I heard someone say,
"She's just an old maid who's gone astray."

Sheridan Homer Isaac Tanner

❖❖❖

Sheridan Homer Isaac Tanner,
A man of renown,
When a boy in school,
Often played the clown.

His teacher tried to quell the habit,
She tried with all her might,
She even tried by giving him
An essay to write.

Sheridan Homer Isaac Tanner,
His teacher to enrage,
Completed the essay and
Initialed every page!

Spreading Cheer
❖❖❖

This is your day! May your wishes come true;
And may your birthday be ideal for you!
May your exuberant cheer take wing,
Soaring higher than the dove,
Spreading hope, and happiness
In the lives of those you love.

Holiday and celebration,
On the day that you were born,
Second baby in the state
On that early New Year's morn.
A precious little girl,
To love, treasure, and adorn!

From my heart I want to say,
Hope you have a happy day!
Never count your candles
Or total up the years,
Ponder on your blessings and
The music of the spheres!

When Skiing Home

❖❖❖

When skiing home across the white,
She thought she saw a fairy's light.
Tall trees cast shadows on the snow,
Blotting the sunlight's fading glow.

She halted there, and pondered long,
And her wish was so very strong,
It conjured up fairies she couldn't see;
Hiding, they fiddled and danced merrily!

As a child, when she passed this way,
Oft she would stop to dream and play,
And pretend to be in wonderland,
Where she danced with fairies, hand in hand.
In her own pretense, she half-believed,
Perhaps desiring to be deceived.

Way up high across the blue,
A sunbeam had filtered through.
The sudden burst of light on snow
Seemed brighter in the afterglow;
And wind whistled through the trees
Uplifting snow with its breeze.

Feeling foolish, on she skis,
Homeward down the trail through trees.
No fairies danced in the snow,
Briefly gusts of wind did blow.

The Fisherman
❖❖❖

By the restless water's edge,
A fisherman sits there,
Casting an eye upon his line,
With a wistful air.

He's half-lounging now,
Under the vaulted sky,
A warm sun upon his back
And white clouds floating by.

Quietly, Fancy comes,
His brow to softly kiss;
She comes to bring him dreams —
She comes to bring him bliss!

Swiftly the waves disperse and
He sees a glorious maiden there.
Her beauty is dazzling —
Though seaweed is entangling her hair.

She carols to him —
She whispers of delight,
And all the pleasures to be had
Under the sea tonight!

She thought she had him then,
And into the water she goes;
That was when the tide washed in,
And he ever had ticklish toes!

At about the same time,
A strong tug on his line,
And a fighting fish — Saved —
From the bubbling brine!

Phantoms

❖❖❖

In every corner phantoms stand
And beckon me with open hand,
When asked if they've come for me,
They hum a quaint melody.

They haunt the hallway and the stair.
When we know it not, they are there,
Sometimes hidden, sometimes revealed,
Then mysteriously concealed.

I think we once knew them all,
If their names I could recall.
They simply slink away and hide
When you are standing by my side.

Reflections of the Past
❖❖❖

Did you look in the looking glass
When you were a wee lad or lass
And wonder from whence you came
Haven't we all done the same

Where did you come from, my dear —
From the past into the here
You got your strength of character, too
From ancestors that you never knew

Oh, the stories I've been told
About life and times of old
Whether or not they can be true
Depends on those you're talking to

Insomnia

❖❖❖

On the other side of sleep,
Quietly, I lie,
Watching light and shadows creep —
Moon-king rides the sky!

Long after moon and stars have set,
Hearing the breezes sigh —
Lying a-bed has made me fret,
Cause sleep has passed me by.

Memories jostled one another,
Leaving nerves taut and tight —
Shoving, pushing against each other,
In a long, restless night.

Birds a-twitter on the lawn;
I've appointments to keep —
But the gentle light of dawn
Is lulling me to sleep.

Old Quincy's Son
❖❖❖

Stars were sparkling in the sky,
And the moon was riding high,
When I glimpsed a man on horseback
Galloping — galloping by.
'Twas old Quincy's son,
Merlin, the restless one.
Where does he go,
Galloping so?
Perhaps to meet a lover,
Or perchance a foe.

Jammin' With the Boys
❖❖❖

My husband plays in the band,
It's something he enjoys.
After hours, they clown around,
And make a lot of noise.

Why do I feel put upon?
His life style annoys!
Out late every night —
Jammin' with the boys?

Saying No
❖❖❖

No is such a little word,
Yet so difficult to say,
To avoid hurt feelings,
We usually say okay.

If the word remains unsaid,
When you want to say "No,"
Just keep a calm and clear head,
Then shake it to and fro.

Her Curiosity

❖❖❖

The neighbor's drapes, as I can see,
Barely move to and fro,
She always peeks out curiously
At those who come and go,
And if anything is going on,
She'll be the first to know!

Her compulsive nosiness
Is the one thing I simply hate,
And oft times she'll exaggerate.

I should beg the woman's pardon,
I impinged upon her rights,
'Twas the southern breeze tonight.

Those Golden Years
❖❖❖

Even though my hair is turning white,
And my skin is not as snug and tight,
Inside I haven't changed a whit,
Although my looks have changed a bit.

I may have shrunk an inch or so,
Into my shoes it seems to go.
I inject myself with Forteo
Hoping a stronger bone mass will grow.

Maybe I am no longer 'hep,'
But I still have pep in my step,
In spite of my aching toes
And ugly compression hose.

Sometimes I sit and read till dawn,
No one to warm my cold feet on.
Only memories share my bed
When I lay down my weary head.

At times I miss a hug and kiss goodnight,
And a special someone to hold me tight.
You tend to forget the woe and tears
When you are steeped in those golden years.

V. Different Types of Poems

A Monorhyme

A mouse caught in a spider's snare,
Squeaked and squealed loudly in despair.
The spider swaddled him with care
In a silken web, fluffed with air.
After she dined she left him there,
Dangling under a kitchen chair.
At dawn, the housewife saw the pair.
The sight was more than she could bear,
And when her husband heard her swear,
He walked into his worst nightmare!
She stood there pulling out her hair
And he was blamed for this affair.

Haiku Poetry
❖❖❖

tree house —
a towhead carves initials
in his leafy fort

one hot summer
violence ran between them —
fueled by sires

wilting wild flowers
found on doorstep —
no one there

moon shadows danced
to the tune of the wind —
on that frosty coast

a golden haze
bathed the mosaic —
misty morning light

rainbow hues
on yon gushing stream —
morning sun

garden flourishing —
veggin' out
packin' calories

drifting
in a shaft of sunlight
golden motes of dust

gray skies
snowflakes melting —
on my tongue

chilly autumn —
a skein of geese
in flight

Summer's Storms

(Double Acrostic)

❖❖❖

Summer's gaudy colors,

Under dazzling sun,

Make senses reel until

Melting day is done —

Errant hearts are beating faster,

Roguish Moon Man may be

Seducing them to disaster.

So much joy — it showed red —

Till cheeks were hot like fire;

Once love and joy were dead,

Rapture turned to sorrow —

Moon madness makes for

Summer's storms tomorrow.

Sunset

(Acrostic)

❖❖❖

She paints with multicolored zest

Upon the lovely evening west.

Now the sky is a purple strand,

She dropped her amber in the sand.

Early pinks and reds are

Turning into stars.

Depiction of Me

(Shape Poem)

❖❖❖

she

thinks she

might want

to be an

artist

someday from

this   depiction   that

she   has made of me   you

may   want to tell   her

that   she will   need

to   practice   if

she wants to

become a great

surrealistic artist

like Salvador Dali

or Pablo Picasso or

Joan   Miro

now   she

has   got

to   be

hell on   wheels

The Crescent Moon
(Shape Poem)
❖❖❖

      Tonight
        the moon
          is an amber
            crescent riding
              high in a distant
                sky. Yet, in a night
                  or two she will turn
                    her full luminous face
                      toward the rolling sea
                      and lure a tumultuous
                      tide across a strand of
                      golden sand and then
                    as swiftly pull it back
                  again, though she
                seems to be fully
              occupied with
            her shining
          light till the
        wee hours
      of night.

Shower Power

(Nonet)

❖❖❖

Rain drops bouncing against each other
above the atmosphere so high —
Lightning flares – "Shower Power."
Expansion of hot air
suddenly explodes —
Thunder crashes,
rolls and roars.
Rain swamps
Earth.

Springtime's Romance
(Nonet)
❖❖❖

The wind whistled a tune at midnight.

Daffodils danced the lively air

with their yellow nightcaps on.

Birds chattered in the trees.

Stars peeked down to see

springtime's romance

until the

break of

dawn.

Diamantes

❖❖❖

Puppy
cute, delightful
chewing, running, pouncing
playful, enjoyable — alert, hunter
sniffing, fetching, guarding
sleek, beautiful
Dog

Rain
liquid, fluid
pouring, drenching, flooding
sprinkle, drizzle — shower, blizzard
falling, freezing, storming
Cold, crystals
Snow

A Rondel

It started with an ardent glance,
With never a thought, I left him there
And gave you my foolish heart to wear,
You were gallant, and loved to dance.

For romance, I gave up the chance
To share in riches beyond compare.
It started with an ardent glance,
With never a thought, I left him there.

With your laughing eyes you'd entrance
A silly girl for sheer novelty,
Or amusement and frivolity.
You must have held me in a trance,
It started with an ardent glance.

Terry's Ballad

(Tune: Amazing Grace or House of the Rising Sun)

❖❖❖

Let me tell you about my grandson
My daughter's only son
Some called him a golden boy
The envy of everyone

He's never met a stranger
If the plain truth be known
He'd gladly give the shirt off his back
If it were the only one he owned

He was named for his father
They say blood will tell
He emulated his grandpa —
He did it very well

Like him, he was a hell devil
Tempting fate at the slightest whim
Once was called a chick magnet
The women flocked to him

Now he wears a wedding ring
That doesn't weigh him down
A son that's his spitting image
The circle keeps spinnin' round

A child was born the other day
A darlin' baby girl
Just one look was all it took
And he'd taken his last whirl

We'll Inherit the Earth
(A rap)
❖❖❖

Carter, Reagan, Regan, Begin
O'Connor, Hinckley, Princess Di
St. Peter's Square, and the FBI
Soviet Union, nuclear arms, AT&T
Senator Edward Kennedy
Reaganomics, Expenditures lurk
Twelve million out of work

007 Flight
ABM, gay rights
Showtime and HBO
Grenada, Beirut, PLO
And effects of El Nino

Bhopal, Mondale, Ferraro
AFL-CIO
Gandhi, Thatcher, Chernenko
First from frozen embryo

Newfoundland, Donovan, Sudan
Ronald Reagan in again
Mexico, Malta, Achille Lauro
Hijacked by the PLO

Chernobyl, Challenger
Space Center Kennedy
Iran-Contras, NSC
Ollie North and his plea

(Chorus)
We'll inherit the earth
So we've been told
As we were growin' old

West German base, three jets collide
Michael K. Deaver lied
Woman leads Pakistan
Debut of Buran

"Ozone hole," Prince William Sound
Exxon Valdez runs aground
Lucille Ball, Panama
Fall of the Berlin Wall

Iraqi rape of Kuwait
TRT, MBB
Redwood Summer, pop sex
Followed by violence next

"No More Cold War!" says USSR
Tailhook, Hubble and the stars
Navajo Nation
Kuwait Liberation

Gene therapy
Housework and infidelity
Bill Clinton, George Bush, Ross Perot
Cheese topped Pizza and voting forms to go

Pot and cocaine on the rise
HIV in paradise
Veggin' means eatin' green
"Alternative" is anything

(Chorus)
We'll inherit the earth
So we've been told
As we were growin' old
We'll inherit the earth
It's our right of birth
For all it's worth

Rodney King and the fuss
Riots in Los Angeles
Smoking, cancer, heart disease
Early death from all of these

Domestic violence out of control
Death of Goldman and Nicole
Barking dog, thumps on wall
Neighbors give police a call
White Bronco ride
Al Cowlings by his side
"The Juice" in trouble — no place to hide

Television, side bars, Judge Ito,
Johnny Cochran and the show
Marcia Clark endures the trial.
Jurors in black set new style.

America's heartland filled with pain
Gathering evidence from remains
Car bomb, nine-story hole
Outrageous death toll

(Chorus)
We'll inherit the earth
So we've been told
As we were growin' old
We'll inherit the earth
It's our right of birth
For all it's worth
We'll inherit the earth
Though we're not really meek
And our future's lookin' bleak

The big freeze, welfare squeeze
Havoc of Mad Cow disease
Economy booms, passengers doomed
Ron Brown, hole in head
No survivors, all are dead

Attention fades
TWA and the Everglades
Palestine, Israel
Unibomber goes to jail

Olympic bomb ruins the day
Life on Mars
Church fires
Death of JonBenet

Mother Teresa and Princess Di
The rich morn and the poor cry
Denver's fate, McCaughey seven
Cult suicide in the name of heaven
Past offering up the sacrificial lamb
Now we've turned to cloning them

Kenneth Starr and friends like Tripp
Country's torn, rip by rip
Investigation, degradation
Clinton won't buy into resignation

Bosnia, Kosovo
Fighting seems to take its toll
Prez impeached
Oprah wins one for free speech
Bono gone
And the beat goes on

Viagra news, cures the blues
Monica yet to pay her dues
Columbine
Makes headlines
Teens scorn
Trench coats worn

Computer infatuation
Guns concealed
Bombs revealed
Healing fund
Reaches 2.3 million

School's out
Followed by drought
What about vegetation
Hoarding food
Taking stock
Pesticide laced generation
Y2K on the way
Loss of young JFK
Good grief, Charlie Brown
Who will lead the nation

(Chorus)
We'll inherit the earth
So we've been told
As we were growin' old
We'll inherit the earth
It's our right of birth
For all it's worth
We'll inherit the earth
Though we're not really meek
And our future's lookin' bleak
Are we on a losin' streak
Or will we be forced to seek
And seek, and seek, and seek...

Party over, things are fine
Still talkin' on-line
Interactive TV
Megamerger history
AOL and Time Warner
Giant backed into a corner
Cost cuttin', choppin' block
Cyberspacin' is the one-stop-shop

Jean Boggs Baker

Will we apply "the rule of thumb"
To the new millennium
What about our conundrums...

Dangers Unknown
(Palindrome or Mirrored Poem)
❖❖❖

Jeopardy and risk

Creating sorrow and collapse

And fear and dread

There's basis for

Unholy awe

Ruin and distress

—Dangers—

Distress and ruin

Awe unholy

For basis there's

Dread and fear and

Collapse and sorrow creating

Risk and jeopardy

Morning

(Pantoum Poem)

❖❖❖

I, who love the morning scene,
Stepped into her early light.
Where dew drops pearl the green,
Breezes whisper in delight.

Stepped into her early light,
Hearing the cock give a wake-up call,
Breezes whisper in delight,
While I tie my hat and loop my shawl.

Hearing the cock give a wake-up call,
Old Hisscat is stalking nearby,
While I tie my hat and loop my shawl,
Watching the fledglings learn to fly.

Old Hisscat is stalking nearby.
I banish the cat, with clicking tongue,
Watching the fledglings learn to fly,
While a mother bird teaches her young.

I banish the cat, with clicking tongue,
   Where dew drops pearl the green,
While a mother bird teaches her young.
   I, who love the morning scene.

Whose Heart Fell Captive

(Sonnet)

❖❖❖

Whose heart fell captive in these hands, and when
Those lips met mine in a lingering kiss,
I pictured your face, and could feel the bliss,
And almost felt that you were here again.
Much of the past had escaped me and then,
Other arms held me with such tenderness,
Easing an anguish laced with bitterness.
All of those lads are now forgotten men,
Like wild flowers on a lonesome hillside,
Where the petals droop and fall and are gone
On an autumn wind; scattered far and wide —
You were my all — our love was lost to pride.
In frozen dreams, your memory lives on;
Hope once lived in me, now that hope has died.

Word Play
(ABC Poem)
❖❖❖

(A to Z)

Auntie, being cantankerous, deemed every friendly gentleman heartless, instantly judging keepers lackadaisical morons, not once pretending qualms. Rather, she tallied umpteen visibly waspish xenophobic yuppies zonked.

(Z to A)

Zany young Xanthippe was very ungracious to Socrates, rudely quarrelling. Pandemonium over nonsensical matters likely killed jovial inclinations. Hurt, gloomy feelings, expressed daily created bitter animosity.

VI. Nature

The Mighty Mississippi
❖❖❖

From a stream in Minnesota,
Just a trickle of shining water,
Millions of years ago,
Became a colossal river,
(Named by Indians, Messippi),
Flowing two thousand miles or so,
All the way from Minnesota
Down to the Gulf of Mexico.

From rain run-off and melting snow,
That small stream of clear lake water,
Accumulated strength and began to grow,
Descending at St. Anthony
Into a turbulent waterfall;
Spinning wheels with falling water,
Generates electric power,
Brightens nights in Minnesota
With its lofty water shower.

A silver stream from Lake Itasca,
Touching ten states, its waters flow,
Muddied by the big Missouri,
The Des Moines, and the Ohio;
From two feet to two hundred,
Reaches the 'Old Man's' muddy floor,
Narrow in Minnesota,
It widens at Cairo,
Some say a mile or more.
All that massive rolling water
Conveying cargo to and fro.

Torrents of rain, and thawing snow,
All of the stormy weather of seventy-three,
Caused the mighty Mississippi
To flood its banks and overflow;
On a wild rampage, the river,
Much farther than the eye can see,
Yanked up houses in Missouri,
And plopped them down in Tennessee.

And down Louisiana way,
Where the great Mississippi flows,
Its deep waters are warm and wide,
Along its banks, magnolias grow,
And the willow trees shade its shore.
Some people like to paint its moods,
Others may come to hear its lore,
Mark Twain would say, this waterway
Will sing a new song every day.

The Storm

✧✧✧

The rosy blush of morning sky
Was lovely to behold,
Awake, the mighty sun reached out,
Gilding the dawn with gold.

It was a picture perfect noon,
No hint of peril — not one —
As evening fell, black massive clouds
Reared round the setting sun.

After sudden lightning flare,
Crash of thunder smote the air.
Wild wind terrorized the clouds before
They opened to let a rain down-pour.

Lightning sizzled, thunder boomed,
A deluge swamped the town —
So many cars piled up
The interstate shut down.

Morning, waking with azure skies,
Rendezvoused with the sun,
The birds with cheerful melody
Declared the tempest done!

Jack Frost

❖❖❖

He came in the evening
As the sun went down,
And all over town,
This glistening little sprite
Draped windows in lacey white,
And brought the gardens down —
Each flower bowed down its lovely head;
Was sweetly caressed until quite dead,
And turned a nasty brown —
Then his naughty mischief done,
Disappeared before the sun.

Lightning

The wind was getting bolder,
Lightning slashed a cloud,
With a roll of thunder —
Not so very loud.

Sunday school was over, and
My child had walked today.
Would she be frightened —
Or would she stop to play?

Concerned for her safety,
As lightning streaked the sky,
Quickly I went out the door,
Hoping she was nearby.

When I saw her she was dawdling,
She didn't seem afraid.
I couldn't help but wonder
What kind of game she played.

With each lightning flash, she'd give a cheer,
And then look up with glee.
I walked up to her,
Curious as could be.

"What are you doing?" I asked,
"And why are you smiling so?"
"Because I'm happy," she said,
"God's making a video!"

The Great Firestorm
❖❖❖

A vast forest covered the hillsides
As far as the eye could gaze,
Until a spark by a careless hand,
Set the undergrowth ablaze!

It billowed when the wind
Fanned its tongues of flame,
Licking at the tree trunks and
Bellowing its name!

Midnight became like day
As flames lit up the sky,
The wind seemed to come in swirls
And how the sparks did fly!

Some passers-by were shaken
And hurriedly called for aid,
Then realizing the danger,
They sent for the fire brigade.

A violent wind flattened the flames;
They plunged to earth in swooping curves;
The air was intensely hot,
A devil dancing on the nerves.

Fiercely they fought the firestorm,
Until every flame was out;
But there'd be another careless hand,
This they knew without a doubt.

Great Balls of Fire

In a momentous event,
On the sixteenth of July,
Astronomers were astonished
By dazzling fireworks in the sky.

Great balls of fire
Over Jupiter were looming,
What scientists called a fizzle,
Began battering and booming.

Pieces of a shattered comet,
The Shoemaker-Levy 9,
Had smashed into Jupiter.
Could this be a cosmic sign?

Will we have a replay
Of what has happened here before,
And be bombarded by comets
As potent as nuclear war?

If vast comets crash on earth once more,
Like those that wiped out the dinosaur,
Kansas is where I want to be,
To buy my property by the sea.

Nature's Wrath
❖❖❖

Nature in all her wrath,
With a roar, hewed a path,

Searing saplings, toppling trees,
Mangling earth, battering seas.

Black clouds cart-wheeled overhead,
Streaks of lightning flashed and fled.

Then as if in regret,
Soaked the ground where she wept.

Winds ceased, violence spent,
Sun lit what nature rent.

A Bird Song

❖❖❖

One morning, by chance, I overheard
The sweet tuneful trilling of a bird.
Half-hidden in the leafy tree above,
Two birds, singing – one to another –
Singing a song of spring? Singing of love?
First, one would trill, and then the other.

They warbled, they quaked, they shook their throats,
Then together, harmonized their notes,
Until the cocky male plied his wings,
Alone, his bereft mate seldom sings.

While listening, I little thought,
What joy their song to me had brought.
Memories that had flown away,
Were echoed in their roundelay.

Indigo Bunting
❖❖❖

Little Indigo Bunting,
In a tree so high,
Sings to his little mate,
Who's nesting nearby.

How many notes do you hear
When he sings so loud and clear?
"See-me, see-me; where-where?"
And then, "Here-here; there-there."

Such a happy fellow is he,
Perched in the tip-top of his tree.
Will he be in such a merry mood
When he has to feed a hungry brood?

That Cat
❖❖❖

A wild thing from the wood,
As black as ebony,
Looked at me with hungry eyes,
Meowing pitifully.

She stared at my repast,
Hoping for a bite or two —
When I held out a morsel,
Her eyes, big as saucers grew,
Then I moved closer
And off the terrace she flew!

Leaving my lunch, I went inside
And watched her from the door.
She scurried back for every bite
And licked her lips for more.

Next day I left some food
Outside on the patio,
That cat invited her feline friends —
Tabby, tiger, and calico.

The Fawn
❖❖❖

Windy weather, damp and drear,
Assailed the early dawn;
Night clouds dispersed,
To show a sprightly fawn.

While his dam grazed, he frolicked and played;
He ran, then stayed; ran again, then stayed;
Until he worked up such a thirst,
That on his mother's milk he nursed.

When some hunter's dog gave chase,
The doe ran with nimble grace;
Fleet from fear, she ran as a lure,
Hoping to keep her young secure.

Across the misty morning light,
The doe was running out of sight;
When his mother could be seen no more,
The fawn's forlorn bleat became a roar.

Alarmed, he crashed into the wood,
And there, on trembling legs he stood;
Feeling fearful about his fate,
Hid in the bracken there to wait.

A Little Pond

❖❖❖

There's a little pond in the meadow
Where water lilies grow,
And blithely birds swoop down to drink,
And shadows shudder so —

Watch out for the little pond in spring
When creeks overflow,
And sliding down the hillside
Comes the melting snow —

And during a hot summer, when
Sun scorches the sky,
You have to pipe the water in
Lest the lilies die!

A Grand Old Tree
❖❖❖

While standing under a leafless tree,
I wondered at its grandiosity,
How it could hold bare limbs so high
Beneath a bleak and dreary sky.
Where birds have flown that nestled there,
It neither knows, nor seems to care.

Summers, in this lovely glade,
Young lovers picnicked in its shade,
Carving initials for all to see,
Marring the trunk of this grand old tree.
Oh, the secrets it has heard
And never once breathed a word.

Clothed in bark to keep warm,
In a harsh winter storm;
It stands majestic and so tall,
And does not even mind at all.
I think, somehow, that it must know
That seasons come and seasons go.

Gusts of Wind

❖❖❖

Wind whistles through the willows,
Shattering the peace at dawn,
Sporadically stroking the melody
Of the tune he's bent upon.

Wind whiffs at the door,
Gusts thrum the windowpane.
Seeking praise for his refrain,
Wind summons clouds of rain.

Springtime

❖❖❖

Hark! The bluebirds blithely sing,
 Welcoming the buds of spring.
 Silver showers make streams sing,
  Melting winter's icy sting.

 Sweet peas upon a trellis climb,
 Where bees tipple time after time,
 And butterflies flit hither and yon,
Until some flowers are chanced upon.

 The little ones are all a-thrill,
  Flying kites on a windy hill.
 Then up comes a capricious wind,
  Tumbling their kites end over end.

 Springtime — when the spirit soars —
  Up and doing out-of-doors,
  All enthused by nature's mirth —
   Vigorous growth and rebirth.

Summer

❖❖❖

Summer is a great enchantress,
Entrancing one and all
With her holidays and pleasures,
To entice and enthrall.

Hear the call of the bobolink
When June adorns the hills with pink,
Or the rat-a-tat-tat in a tree,
And the bees buzzing in ecstasy.

Through a field of new mown grass,
Water flowing clear as glass,
In the creek where children swim,
Hanging their clothes from a limb.

Gaily little bare feet run
In the twilight just for fun,
Catching lightning in their jars,
Fireflies glowing like the stars.

Nocturnal strolls — summer flings,
Love, romance, and wedding rings;
We savor these moments, one by one,
And are delighted with summer's fun.

When a cooling breeze softly sings,
Summer spreads her lofty wings,
Sadly waves her good-byes,
And, then — away she flies!

Autumn

I love the purple hue of autumn,
And an Indian summer day,
Watching the deer in the meadow,
When they come to eat and play.

Little ones hurrying home from school
Think — playmates, holidays, and books.
First, some milk and gingerbread,
Then it's fishing poles, bait, and hooks.

On some crisp autumn night,
When the harvest moon looks down,
You may hear a hunter's horn,
And the baying of his hounds.

Our trees get all decked out
When the air is brisk and cold.
First frost wraps the hillsides in
Blankets of scarlet and gold.

Autumn Leaves

❖❖❖

In scattered showers of brown,
Wind-swept, they fluttered down,
Whirling, twirling all around
Till they blanketed the ground.

Autumn leaves were raked into a pile,
Where little ones tumbled for awhile.
When the children tired of their play,
The leaves were bagged and hauled away.

The trees stood tall, close together,
Bravely facing wind and weather.
They're not aware, nor would they care,
That their limbs are now stark and bare.

Winter

❖❖❖

'Tis the season of delight,
Snowflakes falling in the night,
Late the sun climbs up to show
Diamonds sparkling in the snow.

Bundled up the children go,
Making angels in the snow.
Snowflakes melting on the tongues,
Of the ones they dance among.

Snow and ice, at nature's whim,
Wrapping the trees limb by limb.
Hear the fire crackle and roar,
Wind is gnashing at the door.

Winter, with its heavy snows,
Longer nights of sweet repose.
All's snug and secure within,
Daylight — shovel out again.

Listen to the hush of air,
Crystal silence everywhere.
Snowbound for another day,
Winter takes the breath away!

That Blast of Polar Air

Feel that blast of polar air
Gloomy spirits everywhere;
All this bleak dreariness, I know,
Will soon be buried under snow.

Lead is sheeting yonder cloud,
Snow will soon be seen;
Happiness that sang aloud,
When the fields were green,
Delights the retentive ear —
Lingers in memory here.

Winter is coming fast,
Warm days are in the past.
Gather round the fire in our dwelling,
For popping corn and story-telling.
Then a night of happy dreams,
Sleeping, while the panther screams.

A Falling Star

❖❖❖

A star when falling from the sky,
Blazed brighter then than ever,
As though the flaring of his light
Could flame and flight dissever.

His celestial friends shone on —
Radiance ripped the realm of night,
And they hummed a mournful tune
Until he flickered out of sight.

If you wish upon a shooting star
When it's through the nighttime flying,
It may grant your wish somehow
Through an agony of dying.

Rainbow
❖❖❖

After a brief thunder shower,
Inspired by nature's mirth,
Rain and sun aligned
Between heaven and earth,
And flung their colored ribbons high
In a marvelous glowing arc —
Behold the rainbow in the sky!

Never another Deluge,
God in His mercy vowed.
A token of God's promise is
The bow seen in the cloud.

A Double Rainbow

❖❖❖

After rain, a sudden sun displays
An arc of colors — reflecting rays —
Where can be found a pot of gold,
According to the tales of old.

And if a double bow be seen,
What could that play of colors mean —
Elves, to perplex and mystify,
Have hidden their gold in the sky?

Thundersnow
❖❖❖

When a freak thundersnow storm
Filled with lightning blast,
Shuts a city down,
It's too fierce to last!

The sky grows bright
And in just a moment or two,
A low roll of thunder and —
Gravity waves are passing through.

Volcanic lightning triggered by storms —
When turbulence is in the sky
And snow is accompanied by thunderbolts
The wrath of God is passing by.

After a late winter storm —
The hail, the snow, and lightning are soon gone,
Wild winter thundersnow
Is an atmospheric phenomenon.

VII. Various Themes

A Friendly Stranger
❖❖❖

When I was out strolling,
Enjoying my day,
I saw a friendly stranger
Sauntering my way.
Was it mere coincidence
Our paths crossed this way?

I looked down and hurried by,
When he tipped his hat and smiled,
I can't believe I snubbed him,
There was kindness in his eyes.
Though I'm well past my teen-age years,
I was acting like a child.

You never talk to strangers,
This, of course, I know,
But this stranger was worth knowing,
Instinct told me so.

I still go wandering,
Every now and then,
Hoping that some lucky day
Our paths will cross again.

Opposites Entice

Opposites entice –
Perhaps a day,
Or maybe an hour,
No staying power!
Like hot sun on ice —
I think they may,
Or by chance they might,
Perish of delight!

Faith
❖❖❖

Faith is like a glow of light
That gives comfort in the night.
In a nook or on a knoll
It will elevate the soul.
It's felt in peculiar places,
By all the different races.
In the coldest of climes,
In the meanest of times,
It's faith that will set you free
In times of adversity.

'Twould be sinful, you know,
To extinguish the glow.
Any, knowing have inferred
Faith is belief in the Word!

Multiple Sclerosis
❖❖❖

I run away to curse and cry,
In my rage against MS,
And even play racquetball,
Trying to relieve distress.

Thus I vent my helpless anger as
She struggles with her pain,
Knowing she will accept her fate
And never once complain.

Be it faulty gene or virus,
No one seems to know.
It descended upon us
Striking a mighty blow.

Maybe my feelings were revealed
By the tear upon my cheek,
When trying to restrain
The words I dare not speak.

I can never fathom why
This was meant to be.
Perhaps she tried to ease my pain
When she said to me:

"Doctors don't know everything.
It may have been God's decision
That I should have two of you,
Though they call it double vision."

Another Birthday
❖❖❖

Another birthday soon will be
Knocking at my door.
I've not as many left to see
As there were before.

When I'm taking my last breath
And the world is spinning —
I will try to think of death
As a new beginning.

The In Between

When I was very young,
Things were seen as black or white.
Life's songs were yet unsung,
So the grays escaped my sight.
Now that I'm no longer green,
I can see the in between,
And each person can be seen
As a mixture of both good and bad,
In a lighter or a darker plaid.

Providence Intervened
❖❖❖

We met by accident,
And stopped off for a drink.
Unrestrained by propriety,
We talked till almost dawn,
Foolishly, pondering, on all things —
Other than the divine —
To it, no thought was given.
Fate was dealt with by blithe unconcern,
And the Deity, silent witness
To our audacious conceits —

Proud, adept, and cool —
Confident of our own futures,
We were in total accord,
And separated with a promise
To stay in touch — by email and phone.
A promise impossible to keep —
For providence intervened
Before the break of another morn!

The Past
❖❖❖

Through old fields of memory,
I ponder upon the past,
Should I let her lie dormant
Lest she leave us aghast?

Dare I look upon her,
Does she have a comely face?
Will she convey delight,
Or divulge a disgrace?

All Alone

❖❖❖

Alone, all alone, in a concert hall
All alone in the throng at curtain call
Oh, how the music thrills the hall
But my heart is not there at all

No, my heart is not there
It is flying elsewhere
Enticed by the melody
To where my soul longs to be

Lured by visions of past delight –
'Neath the dome of star-studded night
To ecstasies when I was young
Where the joys of my life were sung

On! My enchanted heart flies on –
To those bliss filled times that are gone

This Once Stately Home
❖❖❖

This once stately home,
By the rippling water's edge,
Where doors stood wide in welcome,
Is standing vacant now —
Time-worn, weathered and gray —
Blistered by summer's sun,
And the frost of winter's breath.

Gone are the lavish drapes —
Tall windows stand agape,
Cobwebs in every corner,
Floors in disrepair,
Music and laughter — no longer there —
The ghostly echoes have departed,
Vanished like a drift of snow.

Negligence, that insidious assassin,
And the seasons, in secret mirth,
Are busy wreaking havoc
On its columns and its roof,
Yet, in rose-scented solitude,
On the overgrown lawn it stands,
Where sorrow lingers in the shadows —
Dreams perished here!

Waiting for Mr. Right
❖❖❖

Wise is she, who walks alone,
But, oh, so lonely and sad,
She sits and dreams of all the things
That she has never had.

Those who smiled upon her, when
She was young and her heart was light,
Were flicked away with a grin,
She was waiting for Mr. Right!

She had seen her sisters' hassles,
So when they urged her to settle,
She fashioned her dreams in castles,
And they hadn't dared to meddle.

Now her head is old and turning gray,
And her days are spinning into night,
But she hasn't thrown her dreams away,
She's still waiting for Mr. Right!

The Prince that she has conjured up
Is like a sunbeam in a cup.
Give her a smile, and save your pity,
All of her dreams are very pretty.

Birthday Wishes

❖❖❖

It's your special day
And though I can't be there,
I'm sending you my love and wishes,
And this little prayer:

May your day be filled with bliss,
And this birthday be your best!
'Twas on a day such as this,
Heaven gleamed to make you blest!

I am glad today's your birthday,
Cause I wanted you to know,
How very much you're cherished
And I get to tell you so!

A Lady-Killer

I thought my man was steadfast,
And would be an outstanding pillar,
I know my Bart has a tender heart —
But the dear man's a lady-killer!

I thought my love was devoted
And truthful as a friar;
But I've caught him in lies that he simply denies
Cause my dear heart's a liar!

My husband loves to dance,
He even likes to waltz —
He dances with the air of a Fred Astaire,
But the dear man proved false!

My lover likes to cook,
He stirs and tastes and even whips up desert;
His food's supreme with herbs and wine and cream;
But the dear foolish man, can't resist a skirt!

Women flock to my intriguing husband,
And at times, I'm perturbed by this —
I've known they'd give all they own
To be wooed by the man I kiss!

My man is an exceptional wooer,
Many have caught his eye;
He'd leave in a minute if his heart was in it —
I could sit home and cry!

Now some will have their nose in a book,
While their uptight husband sleeps,
And some still yet will plan and fret
And watch as the clock's hands creep —

My love is a trifling rover,
Wild and fiery and fickle and bold —
Better my head rest on a faithless breast
Than in a bed that's loveless and cold!

Every Young Girl's Dream

He was every young girl's dream —
Captain of the football team,
Courageous, daring and bold;
Big brown eyes with specks of gold,
And hair as black as night.
She held an apple, rosy red,
And offered him a bite.

When her father heard of this,
It turned his blood to water.
No one was good enough
For his darling daughter!
"Trash of the county," he slurred,
"Scum of the earth," said the old grandfather.
Believing the ugly rumors they heard —
With this boy — they wondered why she'd bother.

His father hung out with unsavory friends
Downtown in a gambling den,
And his mother looked for monogamy
In the arms of other men,
So how could the son be other than
A perversely wayward boy?

Any girl foolish enough to fall for him
Would be courting ruin for joy.
The girl sprang from a pious race,
She'd protect her innocence,
Though oft she flirted with disgrace.
If the boy held her heart enthrall,
It would be as a whim — that's all —
His interest was in the derring-dos,
Not the sweet little goody-two-shoes!

A Spectral Light

❖❖❖

On a windy knoll below the mountains
Between the forks of West and Mud
There stood a weathered cottage
(In the time of long ago)
On dark nights from its windows
A spectral light would glow

'Twas said a headless woman
With oil-lit lamp and broom
Restlessly paced the floors at night
Circling from room to room
In that chilly midnight air
How her skirts did flow and flair

One dark wind-swept night
Some curious, idle men
Took an ax to her door
And bravely staggered in
What happened — no one knows —
They were never seen again

Birthday Celebration
❖❖❖

Let's celebrate your birthday, Lori,
In the grand old-fashioned style,
With warmth, light, and happiness,
And good friends to make you smile.

You bring an inner glow of joy
To each life you touch;
And just for being you,
You are loved very much.

Thank you for all you do, and
Showing that you care,
You have enriched my life,
Just by being there!

With Age

❖❖❖

Leaves turn gold in an autumn sun
As roads are traveled one by one.

With age, gentle days move on,
Then comes the cold winter dawn.

Before winter's snows come to stay,
Treasured moments are tucked away.

Snow-clad paths are short and sweet,
When you have wings on your feet.

Because

❖❖❖

Because your smile is sweet and slow,
And your eyes are a dazzling brown,
My heart is filled with hope again — but, oh!
How I fear you will let me down.

So lay your cards on the table, and
If I sense they signify pain,
I'll leave you to 'Lady Luck,' my friend,
And flee on the earliest plane.

Nostalgia

❖❖❖

I am steeped in dreams of yesterday,
When my heart was young and full of sass —
Longing for the church of my childhood
And its cherished window of stained glass.

For the shouting and the laughter,
My heart is yearning so —
For sleigh rides down the hillside and
The footprints in the snow.

At molasses making time,
My desire's a starry night —
Where I ate skimmin's from the pan
By a wood fire burning bright.

I have a yen for the
Scent of meadows newly mown,
For a glimpse of the old homestead —
All the things that I have known!

I miss the bevy of peacocks
Strutting past the garden wall,
And toward twilight time,
The whip-poor-will's lonesome call.

I am haunted by rolling hills and
The beauty of wild flowers there,
The sweet tune of a bird in flight —
Enchantment lingers in the air!

Should a little glimpse of things past
Matter more or less to me,
Than knowing what the future holds
And the wonders I will see?

INDEX OF FIRST LINES	PAGE
A feisty little old lady named Lou	61
a golden haze	124
A lovely girl	38
A mouse caught in a spider's snare	123
A star when falling from the sky	178
A vast forest covered the hillsides	160
A wild thing from the wood	166
After a brief thunder shower	179
After a flood one winter morning	75
After rain, a sudden sun displays	180
Alex knew much about our presidents	48
Alone, all alone, in a concert hall	194
Another birthday soon will be	190
Around a roaring fire	92
At the time he could hardly believe	12
Auntie, being cantankerous	149
Because your smile is sweet and slow	205
Born a Wednesday's child	57
By the restless water's edge	110
Carter, Reagan, Regan, Begin	136
Champagne Wishes	22
chilly autumn	125
Curse, cry — languish — wait	3
Did you look in the looking glass	113
drifting	125

INDEX OF FIRST LINES	PAGE

Echoes of the past haunt me now and then 17
Eight years old — and she could go where she would 88
Even though my hair is turning white 119

Faith is like a glow of light 187
Feel that blast of polar air 177
From a stream in Minnesota 153

garden flourishing 125
gray skies 125
Gypsies came to our farm in the fall of the year 98

Happy dreams, little one 39
Hark! The bluebirds blithely sing 171
He came in the evening 157
He was every young girl's dream 200
He won his first bowling trophy at age eight 30
Hers, the hands that tended us 28

I am steeped in dreams of yesterday 206
I love the purple hue of autumn 174
I put my first love on a pedestal 19
I run away to curse and cry 188
I thought my man was steadfast 198
I, who love the morning scene 146
I will always remember 83
In a momentous event 162

INDEX OF FIRST LINES   PAGE

In a swimming pool, on a bright summer day 43
In anticipation 25
In every corner phantoms stand 112
In scattered showers of brown 175
In the early morning cold 86
In the early morning light 47
In the elegance of old Charleston 64
It started with an ardent glance 133
It's baseball season again 45
It's that time of year again 72
It's your special day 197

Jeopardy and risk 145

Leaves turn gold in an autumn sun 204
Let me tell you about my grandson 134
Let's celebrate your birthday, Lori 203
Like most young girls of a certain age 105
Like yesterday, I remember 62
Little Indigo Bunting 165
Love's stealth caught me by surprise 4

Money was scarce and I 40
moon shadows danced 124
My family was outside 82
My Grandson took a new wife 32
My husband plays in the band 116

INDEX OF FIRST LINES ....PAGE

My son loves bowling 46
My son-in-law is a man among men 14

Nature in all her wrath 163
No is such a little word...117
Nothing's as sweet as a secret romance 6

On a cold and snowy December day 68
On a windy knoll below the mountains 202
On his way back from the Temple of Doom...................... 78
On the other side of sleep 114
one hot summer 124
One morning, by chance, I overheard 164
Opposites entice 186
Our coal mining heritage 31

Please, oh, please leave on the light 104
Puppy 132

Rain 132
Rain drops bouncing against each other 130
rainbow hues...124

she..128
She paints with multicolored zest 127
She stood before the church of her childhood 26
Sheridan Homer Isaac Tanner..106
Stars were sparkling in the sky 115

INDEX OF FIRST LINES .... PAGE

Steeped in solitude, I write this loving accolade 16
Such an exotic party night 103
Summer is a great enchantress 172
Summer's gaudy colors 126

The chill of age is on him 33
The fool looked me straight in the eye 18
The man who loves me 20
The neighbor's drapes, as I can see 118
The night is cold and gloomy 27
The rosy blush of morning sky 156
The wind was getting bolder 158
The wind whistled a tune at midnight 131
There once was this couple 8
There's a little pond in the meadow 168
This I say, and have said before 21
This is your day! May your wishes come true 107
This once stately home 195
This tale is about my Uncle Clay 79
Though she is a tiny lass 42
Through old fields of memory 193
Tonight 129
tree house 124
Trent is an outgoing, sunshiny boy 56
Two sisters playing 90
'Tis the season of delight 176

INDEX OF FIRST LINES	PAGE
Up before the crack of dawn	29
We met by accident	192
What dreams do you hold	44
When a freak thundersnow storm	181
When I adopted Anna Lee	7
When I was feeling down	10
When I was out strolling	185
When I was very young	191
When my daughter was little	70
When skiing home across the white	108
Where's that little towhead	37
While hanging clothes on the line	66
While standing under a leafless tree	169
Whose heart fell captive in these hands, and when	148
wilting wild flowers	124
Wind whistles through the willows	170
Windy weather, damp and drear	167
Wise is she, who walks alone	196
With head held high, midst whispers false or true	23
Working for the FBI in '54, and	80
Your warm heart — so loving and giving	24
Zany young Xanthippe	149

CPSIA information can be obtained at www.ICGtesting.com
Printed in the USA
239094LV00001B/2/P